SONG OF THE SPIRIT

Reflections on the Character of God in Man

George Lowell Tollefson

PALO FLECHADO PRESS

Copyright 1987 George Lowell Tollefson

All rights reserved

ISBN: 978-1-952026-07-2

Printed in the United States of America

Palo Flechado Press
Santa Fe, New Mexico

RELATED WORKS OF A PHILOSOPHICAL NATURE BY GEORGE LOWELL TOLLEFSON

The Thinking Process
The Limits of Reason
The Immaterial Structure of Human Experience
A Healer of Nations
Unbridled Democracy

Extracts from *Unbridled Democracy*

Spirit as Universal Consciousness
The Thinking Arts
Ethical Considerations
Moral Democracy

For Loretta

Song of the Spirit

I am the image of God. Therefore will I sing, though the whistle of spring is confined in the dying breast of a bird.

I sing the poet strong; I speak to worlds of men, where God has made a song and lifted up one heart that all may learn of Him. Lay down the tools of war; put aside the sword of commerce; learn to plow those fertile fields that will yield the richest grain. Man is spirit, and his harvest is within.

God is that love of life that wells to foam inside our hearts and makes the day grow hot with light and sensual longing. He is the poet's and the lover's friend, the hater of all cold and lifeless forms.

Man is the afterthought of God: a glistening drop of inspiration concealed within the vapors of a soul.

George Lowell Tollefson

The world was made round and man placed on the outer skin that he would have no excuse for claiming he was shut up in a box. But, alas, he has taken the envelope of stars and wrapped it round his stopped ears. With lowered eyes, he mutters in the dark and the cold. He listens not, neither hears.

Summer smoke ruins the clear air, as a languorous haze overcomes a more severe reflection. Rest not the weary eye in easy dreams of peaceful slumber, lest the sentry nod and fail to call the hour of his passing God.

Let us come before God, neither as sinners nor saints, but as men. For it is the nature of evil and good, when in hearts that are neither or both, to be displeasing to the Lord.

An acceptable truth is that it lies within the capacity of man to put aside the reward of merit and any consideration thereof, while persisting in pursuit of higher laws.

The excessive and outworn secularism of our time must pass. A faded rose does not remain on the stem but gives its fallen petals to the nurturing humus of future growth. Prophets of Spirit will arise, like young plants, and the verdant renewal of that age will perfume the air of new summers of delight.

The earth will someday ring with an accolade of joy. Let us advance to that music now so faint, that will in better times give true measure to the seemly dance of enlightened men.

Is it not strange that the bird who must die never sings of death? But man, who is immortal, is ever at pains to clutch at a moment, which belongs to no one but God. Know, then, that the forgetting of our fears is the sole business of living.

Deliver up all things that are not in the storehouse of strength; release the ugly waters of fear. Let them roll into valleys of indifference to fall softly beneath sands of new cleansing. There in the hollow of fresh winds, where the voice of our God tingles like a lark blowing free, we can see that the bending of grass, giving way to more vigorous thought, uplifts by a gentle submission and gives wings, stripped of fetters, to the soul.

Listen to the voice of God, and you will hear a sound so still that the roar of silence closing in will all but obliterate the noise. The best way to listen is to close the ears of thought and hammer down the lids of looking, until a tiny trickle of spirit whisperings tickles audibly along the cold, damp walls of inner knowing.

Will God return to man and resurrect his soul within? We, who pupate now in this unpleasant season, await, oh yearn to see, the change! Our wings are folded of a substance yet unformed.

Sound a trumpet in the ear of time. Make all the world awake and sing of that unmoved and moving thing that never dies within.

Forswear the lasting form of mortal limitation; forget that aught but God is lasting true. Turn the eye within the breast and sense the soul's expanding trust. "I am," it says and thus declares that blossoms on a rose and thorns alike are compact of one root and bush. The soul of man is but a twinkle in the fixed and ever turning eye of God.

We take to troubles when we sleep too soundly in the midst of day. Awake, arise, light the mind afire with thought and myriad questionings! Let the slumber of lethargic men row their spirits into rougher seas. We flow to land, moving upward to the highest peak, where the air is clear as sunlight poured out wet upon a virgin snow.

Oh, Lord, put joy where fear did live. Out of this rent of earth, let the seed spring forth that is a comfort and a shade to men.

We all worship the same God. Yet, like twin saplings reflected in one pool, we break the smooth surface to catch a fragment of ourselves.

The face of rock, sometimes smooth, often coarse or craggy, gets its texture when the wind and rain, winter, and the seething sun do each commune with the special nature of its inner core. Such a dialogue has shaped our many faiths. Is it any wonder then that light reflects from us in different ways?

The voice of man is crawling reason, mounting slowly the high and craggy ledge of vision. The chill of mountain morning and vaporous clouds meets him there. Transfixed in clinging perspiration of such dew, he floats, his mind dislodged from everywhere. He hears his God.

George Lowell Tollefson

In the sound of geese one can almost hear God's awkward voice: free in wild and unmelodious joy.

There is a god in man, swelling full to distended might of fractured phrase. The semicircular utterances of Spirit do compose the full-rounded awareness of a soul.

What does any man know of truth lest he have it? Can a mirror reflect an image it has not taken to its heart? We are the reflection of God, Whose Spirit is ineluctable light.

God is not the Lord of man but of individual men. For a single soul, shut up within his private universe of perception, cannot imagine a larger state of things. So the Lord, in His kindness, has set Himself up within our hearts, that we may easily find Him within a narrow sphere of understanding. Let us then, since we cannot see into the heart or vision of another man, not presume to give him knowledge of his God, since it will suffice both his need and ours if we but point him toward himself. God's infinite domain converges in each single man, whose universe He lights.

God is a fluid. Like water flowing downward in the earth, He is drawn to us. Extending Himself, He trickles thin through the stone pores of our logic, embracing contradictions, good and evil, love and indifference. He stretches, going beyond the incredulous mind, impinging upon His own universal laws, yet without appearing to do so. For He is undivided, never broken, and, like a pool, is gathered into the solitude and quiet of Himself.

We do not position ourselves in relation to God, for we can neither posit a gap nor an enclosure of Him. The Spirit of all things is in the rustle of grass, where the grub beneath the root, unseen of the world and unseeing, takes a sounding of truth. We get the measure of the expansion of heavenly winds in the tremor of earth.

The illusion of refraction—a stick bent by water—is of the nature of our off-centered comprehension of the soul. For, when peering directly into ourselves, we catch a fleeting glimpse of the truth, as it slips obliquely from our grasp.

Truth is infinitude discovered in a jewel of limitation. It is the fruiting tree held in the heart of one seed and the sparkle of worlds within worlds glistening from a dewdrop suspended on a web.

George Lowell Tollefson

✦ ✦ ✦

The eye of God never blinks. For it admits no foreign object which is harmful, nor fears to witness any thing.

Is there cause for lament that the sun will not shine when the stars have left their posts and scurried into morning? Neither, in the bright light of our living, should we conclude that the night from which we came is a signal of eclipse. For though dark should prevail for a season, it will lift, as gathering clouds do surrender their might to a breeze and the expansion of blue.

The iron rod of God, the flashing wire of Spirit, sparkling in the sun like a fencer's foil, pierces the heart with a clean, incisive thrust. We do not perceive the arrival of truth. It does not rumble into view like a train, spitting smoke and banging iron against rail. Rather are we made aware of a change in ourselves, a sudden straightening of coiled springs in the soul.

The greatness of man lies in his sonship to God. For do we not see that the wise who sojourn among us are like an arrow which passes through the shield and heart of an opponent? With the subtlety of Spirit they do pierce and lay waste the carnal implications of unillumined minds.

The highest service to the Spirit of God lies in the will to be free. For it is a gift, not easily accepted, but widely proffered by the father of men. Would He who has set all things in motion, from butterflies to spiraling suns, give to that quickened and most perceptive piece of all matter the duty of becoming a slave?

The hand of God is not uneven. Nor does it betray us with unpleasant surprises. For it is the gentleness of His love which places us at birth upon the soft bosom of a mother. But it is the contrariness of man to push away and seek a storm in the summer. We are only delighted when happiness is uncertain, for we would possess it of ourselves and not of another.

God is both existence and nonexistence, the sliver of light that falls between the polished boards of understanding.

God encompasses all things, but only one thing encompasses Him: trust. It is not what we will but what we dare that forms for us the lineaments of His façade.

George Lowell Tollefson

God is faith. Thus does every man worship as he lives, for living is an act of faith.

One pinch of chickadee dispute compounded by a dozen is song enough to make a chord and run a string of melody. Thus it was at first the notion of our God to fill the tree of earth with babbling tongues that one clear love of Him, many sided, might abound.

The apportionment of our commitment is in thirds. For there is that which pertains to God, a portion to our neighbor, and the rest to ourselves. But these segments of responsibility are not mutually exclusive. Rather they are three facets of one crystal, and the light from any one of them passes through to the others in such a manner as to illuminate the whole.

How shall one know his Lord? When death comes to the door, curtsies, and leads a shattered being off, the God, which is the man, remains.

We are born into a sleep of blazing lights, hardly cognizant of our true selves, until we learn to dream of God.

Song of the Spirit

A moment out of time we are. You can find us like a focus in a corner of this world, but the world dissolves and we remain.

We do not choose to walk with God. But we may wish to stray from Him. A stormy petrel, seeming lost at sea, troubles least about the tossing waves. It will rest in the foaming hair of the ocean's white and angry beard. For it must hear the awful beating in that dear and wrathful heart to live.

The upright heart makes war on God. We must storm the gates of Spirit, curse the Lord, before the blinding silver-sheen of doubt diffracts, dissolves into a flow of unresisting light to bathe the well-made wounds within our souls.

Truth is a well. To reach the life-giving waters, we must descend as though into hell, then, through much effort and a straining of one's back, draw the shining liquid up.

The apotheosis of fear will not raise a people to courage. Neither is strength drawn from the sinews of worry. He who, casting his glance all about, sees nothing but enmity in men shall tremble before a God hard and cold, whose glacial advance leaves a wreckage of stone for a path. But the triumph of trust in the hearts of the bold mounts the high, winding trail of inner peace. Man is an Indian, equipped with llama and flute, whose national song must be lonely, self-sufficient and pure to endure.

The idea is God's gift to mankind. Squeezed out of a blossom of growth and mental tenacity, this tiny drop of earth, welded to air by the water of discernment, sparkles in truth. It is not veracity itself, any more than food is the man; but where is the young bee without its provision of honey? Truth is a soul nurtured in thought, sprung from deep struggle, and pared to its strength.

God's Spirit is a garden we each fear to enter, because we cannot hear its singing birds until we have gone far enough to lose our way in a pleasant meadow.

The Lord is most delinquent in giving advice. He will not stoop to discussion, which is the means by which men fill an ear with the meaningless prattle of opinion. Without direction, in its season, the flying ant also swarms the air.

Song of the Spirit

The provision of the Lord is succinct, a close-fitting girdle about the loins of expectation. The honeybee hones the hexagonal cell to the contours of need. For an economy of motion and use is delicately poised in the providence of God.

The ear of God is deaf to all but sincerest prayer. Unless the song of heart is plaintive, deep and true, the Spirit is a cord, a violin string, that will not resonate to such a plain-sung tune.

The sunrise of virtue will come; the long night of dissipation will fade. The few shall triumph, as is their right, and the many shall learn of their ways.

The fogbound head of man seeks a word with God. But the clear, ethereal star of truth shines far away. Seen through mists, it seems but a fading pinpoint to our unpracticed eye.

The soul and the will are not one. The latter is wild hair and the former the combing thereof.

A razor clam conceals within a shell the softness of itself and sinks it deep in sand. In like wise is Spirit truth folded once within our hearts then put out of mind.

In no light consideration of our need has God made note of human fear. As we deceive ourselves, undo our friends, betray His trust, He lightly sets a thought within: The path I walk is long and heavy borne when I would carry walls to shield me from an unknown siege.

Know that a candle, once lit in the mind, sets its flame in the heart. We are altered in the apprehension of any truth, as a metal changes color in a fire.

There is an impulse in the race of man. It is akin to truth and will raise him from the earth. The birth of God in the flesh, many formed, is the resurrection of which we have heard.

It is God's will that man be set free. But we so love our chains, that we fear lest a weakness be found in one of the links and we should be most ungraciously informed of the matter.

Like a young bird perched upon the edge of his nest, like a young bird who has not yet learned to fly, we pause in the midst of that stride which would take us

Song of the Spirit

from the region of doubt to the sacrifice of fear. For we hesitate to lay aside ourselves in the interest of an indwelling power, which, like a bright flame without smoke, burns clear and unimpeded in the ethereal domain of our triumph.

We fear to venture forth where hope would convene a meeting with the soul. Summer air does also tiptoe in in spring as though it were a blustery wind and knew not warmth would greet it there.

Behold the temperance of God. He burnishes steel with a rough-edged stone; He harvests a purity in strength from the trials that we bear.

We are ever brought to trials by He who loves to stretch the human will until, having nearly lost elastic pull, it firms itself and gains a longer reach.

The trial of our strength is unendurable, yet the bowstring of life is drawn taut to keep the arrow from faltering upon its journey.

The weight of doubt is like a tank, which seeks to crush the enemy. But the will to overcome digs a deeper foxhole.

George Lowell Tollefson

All of trial is to teach the creature where to seek its home. Its home is self, like a star, immutable, precise and fixed.

As the withdrawal of a storm shatters light into color, so the thunder and roar of inner struggles break the placid mirror of our indifference into sparkling jewels of heightened sensitivity; and we perceive that, where matters had seemed all of one hue, they were really many-faceted.

The tallest masted ship at sea never tore a star from heaven. Our highest aspiration will not dislodge the hope that guides us.

One is always climbing the steep hills of faith. It is tiresome, frustrating, irritating. Why not throw the whole business down a well and accept nothing that cannot be seen or felt? But, alas, someone would draw up the bucket and remind you of your thirst.

It is an unacceptable truth that the twin chasms of arrogance and fear leave such a narrow ridge for human nature to stand on, that faith is rendered a mighty effort.

Song of the Spirit

Yet those few who have held this summit for awhile do assure us that in time the ground so swells beneath their feet that nothing can remain of any former misgiving.

Faith is knowledge of a higher order than cognition. For while the eyes can convey the figure of a man to us, or reason his character, only trust can give us an understanding of his worth.

Faith is the ability to be at peace in the presence of doubt. It is not the overcoming of doubt, the assertion of a conviction in the name of belief, stubbornly resisting thoughts to the contrary. For such a tour de force of will results only in an exhaustion of spirit. Rather it is that rest which is found in the quiet, simple trust given to a friend, who is assumed to know best how to dispose of the matter.

A leap of faith is not a plunge into hope against reason. Rather, it is the most reasonable of actions. For it acknowledges the power of experience to confirm our finest intuitions.

Faith is stronger than knowledge. That is why it is given to fish to hover in water with effortless ease, never pondering the science of an inner hydraulics that balances the sea to their will. Men are like fish, until shorn of their fins by a love of speculative control. Then the sea of events and the bladder of thought never coincide in the surge of a harmonized motion.

We do believe what is proximate to sense, adjacent to interest and consequent to thought. But faith is none of these. It is more akin to the substance of being, which is held to be so without cause.

Faith is the Spirit of God. It is not simply His work; it is His nature, His being. For faith is trust; and to trust someone is to respect them, to hold them in high regard. This regard is love of the kind which only God possesses in His nature, for it sees all things in their proper station and does not lift one above another in esteem. It is for this reason that we wait upon God for the seed of love, which is faith. For man, being blind to the whole, sets one part against another in his heart and lays up malice as a bulwark against assault upon the fierce rage of his desire.

The fear of the Lord is a just regard for the inscrutability and wisdom of his ways. It is not a distrust of his concern for our well-being. For it is man who has given perversity notice that it may strike where it wills, like lightning in a forest. But it is the intention of God that every tree should grow unmolested in fulfillment of its being.

Song of the Spirit

Evil is the undesirable option of a free will. It is clouded vision, the mistaken embrace of an anarchic sway over the steadfast affirmation of good in an independent soul. It is the seed of the wild daisy, fallen beneath a bush and sprouting in cold twilight, instead of laughing in the sun.

Know that God is in the place of seeing. To shave the prodigal eye and give a narrow, sharper vision is the work of Him. From within, He planes the soul and moves the variant strains of will in a close, compact articulation.

The darkness of one man's hope is the light of God's desire. For the anxiety of our Lord is inclined toward the voice of pleading aspiration. The wind of His listening whispers along the face of the rock and searches out every crag of disappointment. Like a fresh sea breeze, He awakens our need; and though we cannot see through morning fogs in the moment of our despair; the wild, wet, reeling gull-cry of our impassioned, half-believing lament pierces through to His ear.

It is not the passion of a sweating heart, nor the blood of a fevered eye that yields direction upon the path of hope. Sacrifice accompanies all but vain endeavor; yet the smooth, unlabored ease of moral flight gets its wings from laughter, joy. The oil of tears is but the balm of troubled minds, self-engrossed.

Like a hummingbird hovering near, God visits decision as a jewel in the air, scenting the sweet nectar of such oblation of confidence in Him. We have only to act of ourselves, praising right, to enter the dance of His flight.

The fortitude of saints is found in the virginal delight of God's Spirit. For the Lord conceals the transparent garment of His love in the heart of the pursuer, where the lewd quest of the righteous unveils the secret of His joy, and hope would sooner pine in an ignominious death than yield an irrevocable passion.

Perfection of spirit is inward, not outward. Not one human being upon the face of the earth can escape from the strangulation of sin—of a lying and deceiving demeanor and the itching crosscurrents of the falsely ponderous ways of insincere men—until all is transformed into a sheet of smooth satin, like the unblemished skin of one body without scars. But the Spirit, honing inward, like a bee to the center of its hive, carries a burden of soft balm and rich nectar fit for the royal introduction of a queen, whom the appropriate season of rebirth shall call forth in due measure.

Song of the Spirit

Observe a mountain which is tall, ragged, made of granite. Upon its towering heights cold drafts shiver the seams in the rock. And at times, as a result of this stress of constant wearing away, great columns of its substance collapse and dissolve into valleys and tumble into fast moving rivers to lie buried in foam. Here beneath the white water in the clear, cold liquid of the high country, the mighty heart of lofty crags comes to rest; and it is like the spirit of man which, having stood upon the shoulders of God for awhile and felt the bright undiluted light of the sun, has suddenly experienced the giving of will, the crash and thunder of broken desire, and sent itself hurtling downward to lie concealed in the torrent of other men's drives.

A man must be true. Though his heart yearn to sing but a single note of all the symphony of life; though such a melody be poor and short, unvaried, so that it sound more like a dirge than joyful song; yet he must straight along the path of his conviction go and labor there till the sinews of his spirit release a burden from his soul.

Patience in adversity, steadfastness when every hand is raised in opposition, every voice a hissing serpent, whispering defeat—this is sacrifice and obedience unto God. For He commands that we look, not to men for subjection, but to the power of that bright incentive of Spirit, which is strength to persevere. Like a cougar in the rugged terrain of his conviction, we offer snarling defiance to those who would unseat us from the dominion of mountain air and a haven of conscience free and clear.

To be weak in the Lord is to be strong in spirit. For reliance upon God is reliance upon our innermost being. Heaven is within us.

Through patience is the edifice of faith built up, and through faith, freedom. Not in the façade of a mere transitory regard for good fortune, but in the carefully laid, close-fitted stones of an impregnable wall must hope be sequestered. For it is the irony of a liberated soul that it must be firmly shackled with an indwelling strength to withstand the buffeting of fortune, to accept the heavy burden of joy. The cheerful hues and manifest delicacy of a butterfly belie its long and coarse sojourn as a worm and its necessary term of confinement in a self-constructed tomb.

The efficacy of prayer lies not in what is asked, but released. For if we seek in truthfulness of soul and unity of heart and mind for what is good, we but touch the hand of God in friendship and give Him scope to lead.

When prayer runs deep enough, it turns up in action, and we oft discover that the conclusion of a problem lay in the original premise of an upright heart.

Can we split the ocean into panes of glass or divide a raindrop into many flat, transparent skins? Neither should we seek to offer God ourselves alone as a motive for His acts.

The gift of healing, borne in God, is the capacity to rise above conflicting views and spread the rays of gentle admonition over every living, warring thing.

Do not think that love is to be found in many caresses or an upholding of desire. For these are but the expression of a heart that is eager and a soul that is wary lest its presence go unnoticed. Love is a singular expression of need without want. That is, it is willing to receive into its wholeness that which cannot add to its measure, and it is willing to give forth abundantly that which can never be lost. For love is like a well which, giving forth water and receiving from the springs of the earth, is never observed to change in the quiet equilibrium of sufficiency.

George Lowell Tollefson

The man who loves God loves with Him, for we cannot truly love but through Him. And that which flows in and through all things, coming out of and returning to its source, is spirit. When we love with God, we are caught in the net of His being.

A reflective heart is the highest form of praise. For when we ponder the mysteries of God, like rivulets of water sifting through crevices underground, we fall in an unhurrying, meandering descent to the bedrock of His will. There, rich in the minerals and traveled lore of an inward journey, we fan out upon the table of truth to form a pool of nurture in life-giving springs.

Like a wild duck in the silent reaches of a marsh, among the cool cattails and the sedge, the meditative spirit finds a refuge in his inner home. God, like the placid waters, buoys him; he feeds upon the verdant nurture of the lulling stream. If greatness were a loud event, it would yet have its origin in this place, where minerals of the enriching current, slow and sure, would focus power in the strengthening wing, until the bird could rise in flight and soar beyond imagining.

Song of the Spirit

The housing of the Lord is the open-aired expanse of a liberated heart. Resting in the certainty of a son who understands the best wishes of his father, we come up shoulder to shoulder with God and remind him of our mutual intent.

True moral conscience cannot be socially induced. For that which impresses itself upon the ethical sensibility by means of the mind is not the same as that which proceeds from the heart. The former is the product of will and environment. It arises from the stress of individual interaction within the social milieu. But the latter is of the nature of understanding, not rational, but as proceeding from the Spirit.

The moral sense, when most acute, is less the world's than God's. It is like the angle of perspective in a painting. The lines of understanding and experience converge at a point where observation vanishes.

The moral imperative of God parallels rather than precedes our decisions and acts. That is, the deepest element of our nature, which is Spirit peering through the window of soul, does not enter directly into our behavior. If we listen to this voice of God within us, we are like a piano tuner who sets his ear to the melody of an instrument he does not touch, that he may bring his own into harmony with it. To get the right pitch, we listen to the promptings of the Spirit, then set the score of our character to play a tune wholly originating in us, yet harmonizing with God.

The heart of morality does not change; but the norms of society, like societies themselves, are a part of the ever-shifting flux of the universe. Moral precepts come and go, but the law of God does not. What is acceptable in one place may be taboo in another, yet all things are the same in the eyes of the Spirit. For the God within us demands reverence for the supremacy of His nature in ourselves and a mutual regard for His indwelling in one another. Thus every contradiction dissolves in the pool of His oneness. For when we see with the eyes of the Spirit, we are no longer bound by double vision. We see that difference is not contradiction and that blossoms sprung from a single root do not bloom in opposition.

A consideration of death is in order, if we would give of ourselves to another. For we cannot know the true measure of life and its pleasures, unless we pit their short sway against the long durance of the grave. Then we see that the shadow of God overarches all things, upholding the self and its lover.

It is appropriate that the four seasons should signify something other than birth, maturity, age and death. For the development of life should lead to something other than a cold, wintry cessation or a cyclic redundancy. Let us propose then that fall should be the first of the seasons. It is the beginning of our awareness of limitation, a shedding of false colors, and a deeper rooting of ourselves in the foundation of our existence. When the winter blasts come, they arise in order to cleanse, sweeping away the last vestiges of our past, and seeping life giving waters into the depths of our being. These waters increase into spring torrents, and an alternation of dark brooding skies and short furious tempests prepares us for the time when, adorned with new raiment, we step forth into the light of flourishing, bountiful life. Here in the summer of rebirth and fulness of growth, we take no cognizance of further changes in season. For the strength of our limbs and the spirit that runs free, like sap in young trees, is only limited or bound unto fruition. Life explodes into life, and immortality shimmers in a blanket of green beneath endless blue skies.

George Lowell Tollefson

A civilization may sleep, but the life of God's Spirit in man never dies. For though the trees stretching over a pond drop their leaves at its center, and the gentle working of the ever-spreading waters stacks them damp, lifeless and brown along the margins of the shore, an upwelling of sap shall bring them forth again in the splendor of a new summer of life. We work, we slave, we die; and the products of our hands and our thought slip imperceptibly into decay. But never has the beating of one single human heart ever ceased, so long as other hearts were present to catch the rhythm and pass it on. The ripple of God's love shudders and trills through the often mute and uncomprehending but ceaseless generations of man. And the banner of his seeing is flown from the heights of our slow resurrection.

There is a wrinkle in the air that turns a leaf a certain way. It is the ripple in the ground that folds some roots into coils. No relation? That is so at a glance. But probing deep into the twist of things, we see that God failed to iron the world out thin. He left a kink here and there, like a smile.

Song of the Spirit

Where there is an ambiguity, it is almost always intended. The Lord put the life of a tree between two surfaces of a leaf, that they might express a single origin and purpose.

That the sun might rise without setting and darkness depart forever from the hearts of men, our God has silenced the laughter in heaven and uttered no sound in the ringing void of His remembrance. A new strength is gathered up in the fibrillating heart of man, as the voice of God's Spirit whistles like a curlew through the hollow chambers and barren fields of our rumored demise. Soon, in a moment of unaccustomed expectancy, the stars of our former lights shall drop from the firmament of a closer meditation. For it is the accident of man to forfeit not one whit of his destiny.

In the rustle of grass, through the unobtrusive tunnels of his private domain a meadow vole wends his way. High above in the hot sun a hawk circles, noting those stalks that move against a rolling green tide beneath the wind. Such is the tension between man and his God, when one would seize the other unawares in an erotic embrace. We must die in the quiet of our days when the Spirit descends.

George Lowell Tollefson

The danger is not that God should lose sight of us but that we should lose sight of Him. Let us therefore resolve not to slacken the pace of our running, lest He get so far ahead and we strain so to glimpse Him, we fail to take note of Him coming up behind.

The heart of man is neither muscle nor spirit but a mixture of both. Hence the blood, which flows through it in a circle without beginning or end, but is always a real and throbbing presence, responding to pressure and ease. We grind out our feelings in the substance of ourselves, while the Spirit of God demurely dips an investigative finger in the vapor of our dreams.

The bewilderment of man is the pleasure of God. For in the confounding of our sense, as a sudden wind throws back the flight of a bird and sets him off course, He reiterates the complexity of His plan and the incomprehensible minuteness of the elements of a moral consideration. Though we posses the faculty of intellectual flight, we must ever measure the currents of spirit against principle and doctrine, as if held aloft upon uncertain wings.

There is no moral impudence like that of a closed heart. Though upright in every civil action, though flawless in the character we observe, the man of bound mind and fettered soul betrays a canker of rot at the root, that will surely wilt the blossom when the plant goes to ruin.

Men are never certain of the presence of God. Hence the assurance that His ghost ever lives. For the shadow of noon, as glimpsed by a flower through the gossamer wings of a butterfly pausing in flight, is evidence of a melancholy beauty that passes through our lives almost without notice. God is the suggestion of strength that comes and goes with each breath.

If we would make ourselves into an image of the Mighty God, let us learn to think. It is an act of faith to let such ripples turn in creative strain against the deadly pull of a falling stream.

We are not the originators of ourselves. Ours is a proprietorship of trust. As the fleeting wind of our souls passes lightly through the forest of our wants, fluttering leaves of inclination sparkling in the sunlight of dreams, we would do well to recall that the voice of retreat shall soon be sounded, when we must withdraw from the ringing plains of this fight.

George Lowell Tollefson

What is duration but a spot in time? He who knows eternity does not speak of it, as two lovers, in a sigh of moans, need no words.

Shall we reappear in another time and place? Will the soul of man, sailing off into the night, reemerge flaming new as does the sun? Perhaps, if God declares it so. It will once more invest itself in the cocoon of life. But what is this to us, if the dying moth should return again to buzz about another lamp? Is not the lamp we have light enough?

In the evening of life, when the smoke of man thins into air, he is most apt then to recall the burning flame that put him here.

Austere is man when he most loves his God. Severe in every aspect of a ritual interplay of mind and heart, he stands aloof from the liquid song of birds and frothy evening sun. The Creator, busy munching grapes and sniffing honeysuckle sweet in a quiet, soft, and breezy corner of a field, feigns embarrassment—sometimes real!—when discovered at His game.

The creed of the ascetic is distasteful to a man of the world, for it eschews the sharp clashing of vain spirits. But it also mutes the exhilaration of spirit. For while it honors the love of a man for his God, it denies the Spirit ample room to sing the song of life in our members. Yes, it is true that, like the wind, we must cease from blowing over the hot floor of a spiritual desert, beclouding our vision with the stinging red sands of vain longings and misbegotten desires. But it is also a truth that when God is within us, He will teach us to list over green meadows of heightened sensual joy and to meander along quiet brooks of natural as well as spiritual reflection. For the earth was made for man and man for the Lord. When we have come into our birthright as His sons, we shall take possession of His estate and glory in glorifying Him through ourselves.

That many can be one without enumeration, and one many without division, is the enigma of God. As the wind shifts the sands of a dune and it flows without the appearance of motion, so the infinitude of divine articulation springs forth in many rivers, which arose from and water the sea.

Made in the USA
Middletown, DE
25 September 2022